Modern Industrial World

The United States

Cass R. Sandak

RSVP
**RAINTREE
STECK-VAUGHN**
P U B L I S H E R S
The Steck-Vaughn Company

Austin, Texas

MODERN INDUSTRIAL WORLD

Australia   Portugal
Great Britain   Russia
Canada   South Africa
France   Spain
Germany   Sweden
Japan   The United States

Cover: The skyscraper skyline of Manhattan Island, home to New York City's financial district

Title page: The stunning landscape of Monument Valley in Utah

Contents page: First opened to traffic in 1931, the George Washington Bridge connects New York City with New Jersey. The lighthouse beneath it was one of the first structures to be built on Manhattan in the nineteenth century.

All map artwork is by Hardlines Cartographers
All graph artwork is by Mark Whitchurch.

© **Copyright 1997, text, Steck-Vaughn Company**

Published by Raintree Steck-Vaughn Publishers,
an imprint of Steck-Vaughn Company

Library of Congress Cataloging-in-Publication Data
Sandak, Cass R.
The United States / Cass R. Sandak.
    p.   cm.—(Modern Industrial World)
    ISBN 0-8172-4556-1
    1. The United States—Juvenile literature.
    I. Title. II. Series.
    E156.S262 1997
    973—dc20   96-8358

Printed in Italy. Bound in the United States.
1 2 3 4 5 6 7 8 9 0 01 00 99 98 97

Contents

The Land and Its People   4

Regions of the Mainland   6

The Country Grows   12

Agriculture, Fishing, and Forestry   18

Trade and Industry   24

Transport and Communications   28

Science and Technology   32

Life in the United States   36

Facing the Future   44

Glossary   46

Further Information   47

Index   48

Introduction

The United States is an enormous country in the northern hemisphere. It stretches for almost 3,000 miles from the Atlantic Ocean on the east coast, to the Pacific Ocean on the west coast. To the north lies Canada, and to the south, Mexico. A distance of about 2,000 miles separates the northernmost point of the mainland in the state of Maine, from the southernmost point in the state of Florida.

The United States is made up of fifty states, forty-eight of which are on the mainland and border one another. These states are called the continental, or contiguous, states. Two other states lie outside this main body: the huge state of Alaska, at the far northwest of the North American continent bordering Canada, and Hawaii, which is made up of a group of islands in the Pacific Ocean, about 2,600 miles from the California coast. Puerto Rico, an island in the Caribbean Sea, is a self-governing part of the United States, with a largely Hispanic culture. Other U.S. possessions include Guam, American Samoa, Wake Island, and Midway (all in the Pacific), and the American Virgin Islands in the Caribbean.

Every U.S. president since John Adams has lived in the White House, built in 1800 in Washington D.C.

The United States was founded in 1776, making it a fairly new nation. Its capital is a city specially built for that purpose: the District of Columbia, also known as Washington D.C. For almost 200 years the city has been the seat of government for the country. There are many large and imposing government buildings in the city, and it is a popular tourist attraction.

Between 250–255 million people live in the United States. The country is so vast that there are four time zones in the continental states alone. For example, when it is noon in New York City, it is only 9:00 A.M. in San Francisco or Los Angeles. Rain forests, grasslands, deserts, swamps, rugged mountains, and prairies are dotted throughout the country. The landscape and climate change from place to place, and even within a single state there can be huge differences in landscape and temperature.

Salton Flat in Death Valley, California, the lowest point in the United States

The Statue of Liberty has welcomed travelers to the U.S. since 1885.

THE UNITED STATES AT A GLANCE

Largest state: Alaska	656,424 sq. mi.
Smallest state: Rhode Island	1,545 sq. mi.
Longest river: Missouri/Mississippi	3,710 mi.
Highest point: Mt. McKinley, Alaska	20,322 ft.
Lowest point: Death Valley, California	282 ft. below sea level
Deepest lake: Crater Lake, Oregon	1,932 ft. deep
Tallest building: Sears Tower, Chicago	1,453 ft. high
Total area (50 states & Washington DC):	3.8 million sq. mi.

Source: Bureau of Census and National Climatic Data Center, U.S. Dept. of Commerce

The National Anthem

Oh, say can you see by the dawn's early light
What so proudly we hailed at the twilight's last gleaming?
Whose broad stripes and bright stars through the perilous fight,
O'er the ramparts we watched were so gallantly streaming?
And the rockets red glare, the bombs bursting in air,
Gave proof through the night that our flag was still there.
Oh, say does that star-spangled banner yet wave
O'er the land of the free and the home of the brave?

—Francis Scott Key, 1814

Regions of the Mainland

THE NORTHEAST

The northeast is made up of six states and is also known as New England, because its earliest settlers were colonists from England who sought religious freedom. When the country belonged to England, it was made up of thirteen colonies. These were all on or near the east coast, since natural harbors, good soil, and a gentle, green countryside not unlike the England that many colonists had left made the east coast a natural home for them. The port of Boston quickly grew to become one the nation's first important cities.

THE TEN LARGEST AMERICAN CITIES, 1990	
CITY (STATE)	POPULATION
1. New York, (NY)	7,322,564
2. Los Angeles, (CA)	3,485,557
3. Chicago, (IL)	2,783,726
4. Houston, (TX)	1,629,902
5. Philadelphia, (PA)	1,585,577
6. San Diego, (CA)	1,110,623
7. Detroit, (MI)	1,027,974
8. Dallas, (TX)	1,007,618
9. Phoenix, (AR)	983,403
10. San Antonio, (TX)	935,393

Source: Bureau of the Census, U.S. Dept. of Commerce, 1990

REGIONS

Northeast (New England)
Mid-Atlantic
The South
South-central and central
Middle West
West

---- State boundaries
—·—· International boundaries

0 500 km
0 300 miles
N

BERING SEA
PACIFIC OCEAN
ALASKA
Anchorage
CANADA
Juneau

CANADA
0 800 km
0 500 miles
N

Olympia
WASHINGTON
Salem
OREGON
IDAHO
Boise
Helena
MONTANA
NORTH DAKOTA
Bismarck
MINNESOTA
SOUTH DAKOTA
Pierre
St Paul
WISCONSIN
Madison
MICHIGAN
Lansing
NEW HAMPSHIRE
VERMONT
Montpelier
MAINE
Augusta
Concord
MASSACHUSETTS
Albany
Boston
Hartford
Providence
RHODE ISLAND
CONNECTICUT
NEW YORK
New York
Sacramento
Carson City
NEVADA
San Francisco
CALIFORNIA
Salt Lake City
UTAH
Cheyenne
WYOMING
NEBRASKA
IOWA
Des Moines
ILLINOIS
OHIO
Columbus
PENNSYLVANIA
Harrisburg
Pittsburgh
Trenton
NEW JERSEY
Los Angeles
Denver
COLORADO
Lincoln
KANSAS
Topeka
Springfield
INDIANA
Indianapolis
WEST VIRGINIA
Annapolis
Dover
DELAWARE
MARYLAND
Washington DC
ARIZONA
Santa Fe
NEW MEXICO
Phoenix
Jefferson City
MISSOURI
OKLAHOMA
Oklahoma City
ARKANSAS
KENTUCKY
Frankfort
Charleston
VIRGINIA
Richmond
PACIFIC OCEAN
Nashville
TENNESSEE
Raleigh
NORTH CAROLINA
Little Rock
Columbia
SOUTH CAROLINA
MISSISSIPPI
Atlanta
Montgomery
GEORGIA
ATLANTIC OCEAN
TEXAS
Austin
LOUISIANA
Jackson
ALABAMA
Baton Rouge
Tallahassee
FLORIDA
Bahamas
Miami
MEXICO
GULF OF MEXICO

HAWAII
Honolulu
PACIFIC OCEAN
N
0 300 km
0 200 miles

Opposite A modern aerial view of Boston, Massachusetts, one of the first big U.S. cities

THE MID-ATLANTIC STATES

The mid-Atlantic region was first settled by people from different parts of Europe: the English went to Pennsylvania and New Jersey, the Dutch settled much of New York, and people from Sweden colonized what is now Delaware.

As in the New England states, good natural harbors, rich farmland, and a relatively gentle climate made the land attractive to early settlers. New York City fast became a major city, a position it still holds today.

THE SOUTH

Farther south, the gentle hills of the mid-Atlantic states give way to the humid, densely green areas of the southern states. These lie between the Atlantic Ocean and the Gulf of Mexico. The land here is rich and fertile, and the generally high humidity keeps the soil moist. It is good for growing cotton and tobacco, among other crops. In Florida the weather is temperate and warm throughout the year. This region is ideal for growing citrus fruits.

THE SOUTH-CENTRAL AND CENTRAL STATES

As one moves westward, the east coast and the south give way to the plains and prairies of the midwest. Through this region, the mighty Mississippi River runs north to south, emptying into the Gulf of Mexico at New Orleans. The river divides the eastern part of the country from the rest. Much of this land is good for growing wheat, corn, and other crops. But about half the land is rocky and barren and suitable only for cattle grazing. When oil was discovered in Texas in 1901, it gave the largest contiguous state a special claim to greatness.

Barges and tugboats carrying freight on the muddy Mississippi. At 2,400 miles long, the Mississippi is the principal river of the United States.

THE MIDDLE WEST

Sometimes known as America's "heartland," these are the great farmland states, where for much of the country's history, wheat and corn have been major products. Michigan and Wisconsin's cooler temperatures and greener land have made them home to dairy farming.

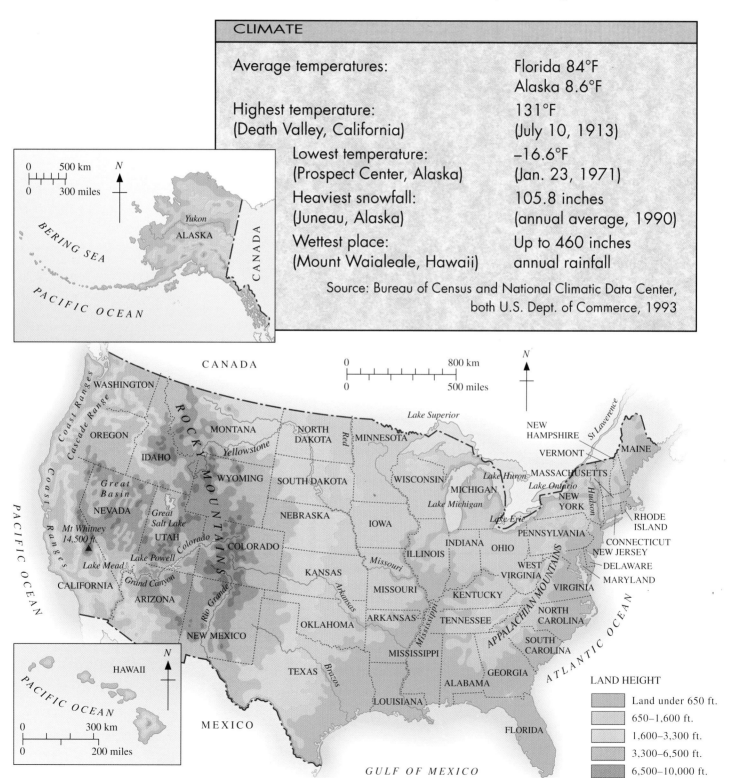

CLIMATE

Average temperatures:	Florida 84°F
	Alaska 8.6°F
Highest temperature: (Death Valley, California)	131°F (July 10, 1913)
Lowest temperature: (Prospect Center, Alaska)	–16.6°F (Jan. 23, 1971)
Heaviest snowfall: (Juneau, Alaska)	105.8 inches (annual average, 1990)
Wettest place: (Mount Waialeale, Hawaii)	Up to 460 inches annual rainfall

Source: Bureau of Census and National Climatic Data Center, both U.S. Dept. of Commerce, 1993

LAND HEIGHT

- Land under 650 ft.
- 650–1,600 ft.
- 1,600–3,300 ft.
- 3,300–6,500 ft.
- 6,500–10,000 ft.
- Land over 10,000 ft.

THE WEST

The Rocky Mountains run north to south through much of this region. East of the Rockies, most river systems empty into the Gulf of Mexico. West of the Rockies, they flow into the Pacific Ocean. Much of the states of Nevada, Utah, Arizona, and New Mexico is desert. Arizona is home to the Grand Canyon, one of the country's most famous and stunning natural attractions.

California's superb weather has made it one of the fastest-growing and most popular states. Hollywood, a part of Los Angeles, became the center of the American film industry. Less than 300 miles from Los Angeles lies Death Valley, the lowest place in the nation. And some 600 miles to the north is a temperate rain forest.

ONE NATION, INDIVISIBLE

The citizens of these six regions all belong to one country, yet their origins may be from all over the world. Most Americans speak English (or American, as it is jokingly called), but for nearly one-fifth of the population, English is not the first language. There are many Spanish speakers, especially in cities and towns along the Mexican border, but German, Italian, French, Asian, and Polish-speaking communities also exist, mostly in the larger cities of New York, Chicago, and Los Angeles.

Opposite Arizona's Grand Canyon, one of the country's most majestic sites. The world's deepest land gorge, it is 277 miles long and an average of one mile deep.

Left In Taos, New Mexico, a pueblo, or communal dwelling, which is over 800 years old.

10

The Country Grows

The first people probably came to North America from Asia, crossing into what is now Alaska over land that once connected the two continents. Many scientists think this took place between 10,000 and 50,000 years ago. Over the years, these people moved through North and South America, many settling in various regions of what is now the United States. Since they did not leave any written records, much of what we know about them is based on objects that have been found buried in the ground.

A petroglyph, or rock painting, drawn by the native Anasazi people over 800 years ago.

EUROPEAN SETTLEMENT

Spanish explorers landed in the area that is now the continental United States as early as the 1500s. It was on the east coast that the first permanent European settlements were made. English colonists landed at Jamestown, Virginia, in 1607, and a few years later a group of English pilgrims, seeking religious freedom, landed at Plymouth, Massachusetts. Soon, people from other parts of Europe came, and the country began to take on the international flavor that it has today.

INDEPENDENCE

By 1775, the colonists were in revolt against the English parliament that ruled them. War broke out—the

Above A historical print showing the attack on
Bunker Hill during the American Revolution

American Revolution—which lasted
six years. In 1776, a group of
colonial leaders wrote and signed
the Declaration of Independence,
which stated the need for freedom and
independence. This document paved
the way for a democratic nation.

Under General George Washington,
the colonial forces fought hard against
the English redcoats. Finally, in 1781,
the war was over, and a new country
had been formed. Between 1812 and
1814, another war broke out between the
United States and England over rights
to the seas. After this the new country
began to concentrate on its
development as a powerful
nation.

Right A statue of George Washington,
the first president of the United States.
He was inaugurated in 1789.

General Philip H. Sheridan and other northern cavalry generals photographed in 1864, during the Civil War. Over 600,000 people were killed in the Civil War of 1861–1865.

Much of the country beyond the original colonies lay unexplored, and there was some doubt as to how much land the United States actually owned. In 1803, the Louisiana Purchase (from France) added more than 770,000 square miles and established western frontiers ripe for exploration. Settlers pushed Native Americans off lands that they had lived on for generations. Frontier towns and forts sprang up as settlers protected themselves against the infuriated Native Americans. By the late 1860s, a railroad joined the east of the country with the west.

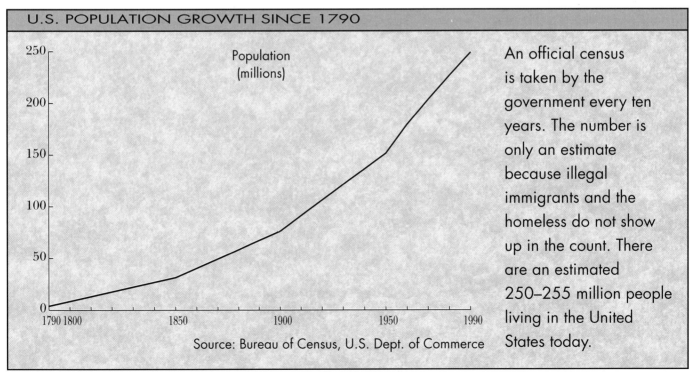

U.S. POPULATION GROWTH SINCE 1790

Population (millions)

Source: Bureau of Census, U.S. Dept. of Commerce

An official census is taken by the government every ten years. The number is only an estimate because illegal immigrants and the homeless do not show up in the count. There are an estimated 250–255 million people living in the United States today.

SLAVERY AND CIVIL WAR

Meanwhile the North and South divided over the issue of slavery. People in the South held slaves, northerners did not. The rural South had used slave labor to work on its enormous plantations since the seventeenth century. The issue came to a head in 1861, when the South withdrew from the United States to form the Confederate States of America. The North was determined to keep the states united, and the great Civil War of 1861–1865 began.

When the war was over, and the Union was saved, the nation continued to develop. About this time, immigrants, sometimes as many as 3,000 people a day, came from all parts of Europe. The country needed workers, and the doors were wide open. People from all nations still emigrate to the United States, but stricter laws now limit the numbers of immigrants permitted.

THE TWENTIETH CENTURY

In the early twentieth century, the United States began to emerge as an international power. World War I began in Europe in 1914, and the United States joined in 1917. By 1918 the war was over, but with a huge loss of lives. World peace returned and so did prosperity for the United States.

An engraving of slaves celebrating, waving copies of President Lincoln's Emancipation Proclamation *of 1863, which banned slavery in the United States.*

Left In the late 1960s, Americans began to protest against the country's involvement in Vietnam, which by 1967 saw almost half a million U.S. troops fighting there.

Below The Vietnam Memorial, in Washington D.C., was erected in honor of Americans killed during the Vietnam War (1964–1973). The names of all those killed are inscribed along the length of the wall.

World War II began, for the United States, when Japanese bombers attacked the U.S. Naval Base at Pearl Harbor, Hawaii (not then a state) on December 7, 1941. With fierce battles fought on both the Atlantic and Pacific fronts, the war was finally brought to an end largely by the threat of an ultimate weapon, the atomic bomb, first used by the United States against Japan in 1945.

After the war, the United States found itself one of the world's superpowers, along with the strong and secret communist Soviet Union. Over the next forty years, the two superpowers competed against each other in a period known as the Cold War. During this tense period, the United States took military action in Korea and Vietnam. The collapse of Communism in the Soviet Union and Eastern Europe in the late 1980s brought the Cold War to an end.

MODERN UNITED STATES

As U.S. power has grown worldwide, much of life in the nation has become more and more difficult. The 1960s introduced protests in which many people spoke out against politicians and role models. Traditional patterns have now changed. The process of urbanization (the growth of cities) has continued. Inflation has meant people can buy less with their money. Established businesses have disappeared, a fiercely competitive atmosphere has emerged, and a new culture, based on the computer, has grown up. As prices have risen, so have poverty, crime levels, and drug use, and the good quality of life, previously taken for granted, has been brought into question and at times even threatened.

IMPORTANT DATES IN U.S. HISTORY	
1607	First permanent settlement founded at Jamestown, Virginia.
1620	Pilgrims arrive on *Mayflower* at Plymouth, Massachusetts.
1773	Boston Tea Party.
1775–81	American Revolution.
1776	Declaration of Independence is signed.
1789	U.S. Constitution adopted.
1803	Louisiana Purchase is signed with France, adding territory.
1812–14	War with England.
1849	California Gold Rush begins.
1861–65	Civil War between northern and southern states.
1914–18	World War I (U.S. enters 1917).
1930s	Economic Depression.
1939–45	World War II (U.S. enters 1941).
1950–53	Korean War.
1964–73	War in Vietnam.
1969	First men land on the moon.
1989	End of Cold War and fall of Communism in Eastern Europe.

"When I was on the police force, the major job was to investigate robberies and small crimes. Everything used to be in downtown areas, but now it's in the wealthy suburbs and high-price parts of town. Now the crimes are big ones, and ugly ones, and race has become a big issue here in southern California."
—Sanford ("Sandy") Lutz, Los Angeles Police Department officer, retired

Homelessness is a real problem today. These two men represent the rights of the homeless in St. Paul, Minnesota.

17

Agriculture, Fishing, and Forestry

Modern agricultural vehicles harvest corn in the Midwest.

AGRICULTURE

When the United States was founded in 1776, over 90 percent of its citizens were directly involved in farming, even if they also practiced other skills or trades. Even as recently as 1950, some 23 million Americans (or 20 percent) lived on working farms. Today less than 5 million, or slightly more than 2 percent of workers, are engaged in farming. Of those 5 million farmers, 48 percent live in the Midwest.

Fertile soil and efficient farming methods—including sophisticated machinery, irrigation systems, scientifically formulated fertilizers and pesticides, and crop rotation—have all contributed year after year to successful harvests. Farms in the United States regularly produce surplus crops that are sold overseas. Farm products total about 8 percent of all U.S. exports.

PRINCIPAL U.S. CROPS, 1993	
	(million bushels)
Corn (for grain)	6.3
Wheat	2.4
Soy Beans	1.8
Sorghum (for grain)	0.6
Barley	0.4
Oats	0.2
Source: Natural Agricultural Statistics Service, U.S. Dept. of Agriculture	

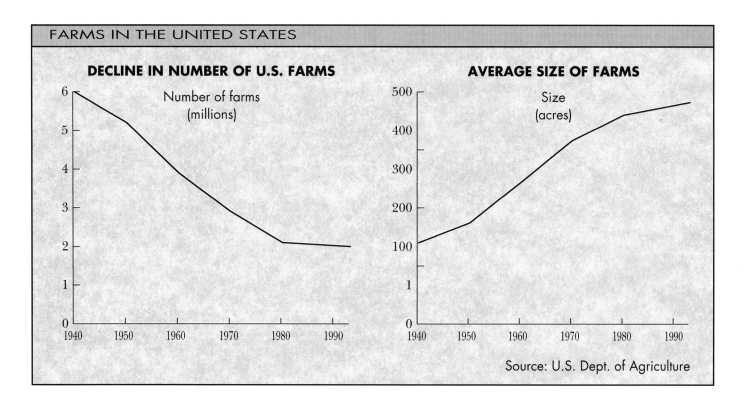

DECLINE IN NUMBER OF U.S. FARMS

Number of farms (millions)

AVERAGE SIZE OF FARMS

Size (acres)

Source: U.S. Dept. of Agriculture

Corn was first cultivated by the Native Americans. About 10 percent is still used for cornmeal, vegetable oils, and other human foods, but 90 percent becomes feed for cattle and pigs.

Florida is the center of the citrus-growing industry. Most Florida oranges end up as orange juice, whereas California, in the West, supplies more citrus fruit that is eaten. The ideal climate of California's Imperial Valley makes this region the supplier of nearly 80 percent of all U.S. fruits and vegetables.

The economic life of the South largely developed around cotton grown on vast plantations. Bales of cotton grown today supply the textile mills around the South and are also exported to developing countries around the world.

A forklift loads crates of oranges from an orchard onto a trailer in Visalia, California.

19

Above *A Texas cattle rancher with part of his herd*

Chicken farming and cattle raising have changed over the last fifty years. To increase production, inhumane methods are often used. Some animals may live virtually their entire lives in cramped cells, injected with antibiotics and hormones to encourage faster growth and higher quality meat. Cattle are generally raised on land that is not good or flat enough for crop farming, but which provides enough grazing for animals. However, it is an expensive livelihood and can be a precarious one; for example disease can wipe out a whole herd.

Subsidies paid to farmers by the U.S. government are less than those paid in many other developed countries. For example, Japan and countries of the European Union encourage the traditional agriculture of their farmers with generous grants and tax exemptions.

Below *Cowboys rounding up horses in Oregon*

"A hundred years ago, this was the way of life of just about everybody out here, but now the working ranches are few and far between. It's barely a viable business anymore. To help make ends meet, my sister and I run a dude ranch in the summer. People come from all over the country and pay money to learn to ride and rope horses. We make almost as much money, and it's a lot more fun!"
—Randa Niles, Colorado rancher

FISHING

Not surprisingly, the fishing industry is concentrated on or near both the Atlantic and Pacific coasts, where the catches are good and where there are supporting industries and businesses that buy the fish. The West Coast, in particular, is a center for fish canneries, where fish are packed into cans.

However, in recent years overfishing, where fish stocks are caught faster than they can replace themselves, has affected the industry. Fish stocks and catches have declined as a result. The lobster industry in Maine, salmon in the Pacific northwest, Alaska's famous King crab, oysters from the beds around Chesapeake Bay, and Cape Cod's fish have all suffered in recent years. More dangerous to the industry than overfishing are the risks of disease from fish caught in polluted waters. Fish farming has become a costly but necessary alternative. These fish hatcheries raise many commercial types of fish to supply restaurants and markets and also provide trout and bass for stocking lakes, streams, and rivers. But the extra cost of fish farming has increased the price of fish and fish products for consumers.

A worker at a crab-processing plant in Alaska

21

FORESTRY

Good forests cover much of the land. Most commercial timber is harvested in the rich forests of the northwestern states and Alaska. The logging industry processes some 19 billion cubic feet of raw timber every year. Most of this supplies the construction industry at home and abroad. Lumber from the South—particularly fruitwoods—is generally used in the furniture industry. Forests of New York State also supply wood pulp for the paper industry.

GIANT REDWOODS

The giant redwoods (or sequoias) of California are huge coniferous trees that live for hundreds of years. Some examples are over 2,000 years old and are so big that a car can be driven through the base of the trunk. The largest redwood, named General Sherman, is estimated to weigh 1,500 tons. Redwood is mainly used for siding (lining the exterior of buildings), decks, porches, and outdoor furniture, since it is a wood that is particularly resistant to weather, fire, and insects.

Opposite *California's ancient redwood, or sequoia, trees*

Below *Lumber on barges in Alaska. The paper mill in the background will process other wood into paper.*

22

Trade and Industry

Inside the New York Stock Exchange, in New York City's famous Wall Street area. The pulse of the nation's economy beats here.

The Gross National Product (GNP) of the United States represents the largest economy in the world. The GNP is a figure that is the total value of all goods and services produced in the nation by U.S. businesses and individuals, including foreign-owned companies. In 1993, the GNP of the United States was $6.348 trillion.

Most American trade is conducted with Japan and its next-door neighbors, Canada and Mexico. Canada is the largest U.S. trading partner. Other markets are found in Europe, Russia, and in many of the developing countries of the world.

After much debate, the North American Free Trade Agreement (NAFTA) was endorsed by the United States in November 1993. This treaty lowered tariffs on trade between the United States, Canada, and Mexico. After two years, it was clear that the giant U.S. corporations had benefited most from the agreement, with profits boosted by cheaper components and manufacturing costs available from Mexico. The nation's 77 million production workers have, as a result, watched their hourly wages drop by 3 percent, and independent public information groups report that in late 1995, nearly

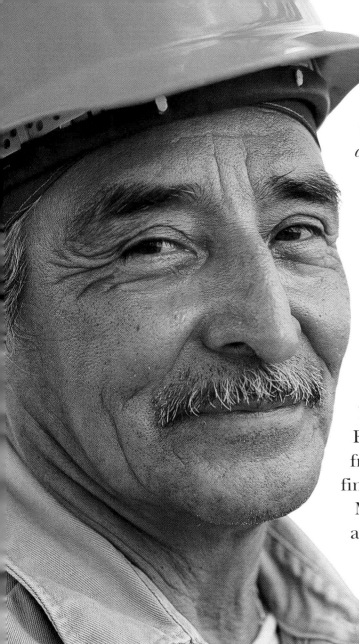

A Hispanic construction worker wearing the protective headwear of his industry, known as a "hard hat"

1 million jobs had been lost by U.S. workers. Even Mexican workers have not benefited from the agreement because of Mexico's financial problems.

Major U.S. exports—in addition to foodstuffs and raw materials—are motor vehicles, airplanes and airplane equipment, and computer hardware and software as well as other office equipment (photocopiers, calculators, and communications systems).

ENVIRONMENTAL DAMAGE

There has been much environmental damage in many regions by short-sighted businesses seeking quick profits. Air, land, and water have been polluted. Sewage, strip mining, erosion, and the dumping of untreated industrial wastes have also had a damaging effect. Acid rain, smog, and dirty waterways that are unsafe for fishing are further environmental concerns.

However, many cities, such as Pittsburgh, have made efforts to deal with environmental issues by imposing restrictions on industrial activities that are harmful. No longer a city famous for its black smokestacks and air choked with coal dust, Pittsburgh has become one of the cleanest, most habitable cities in the United States, with a rich cultural life and strong civic spirit.

STEEL AND COAL

Steel production in the United States was traditionally concentrated in Pittsburgh and the Great Lakes region, because these parts of the country were near the iron ore and coal needed to make the steel. Water transportation for shipping was also readily available. Anthracite, the hardest coal, which burns at the highest temperature and with the lowest waste, also comes from western Pennsylvania. Other rich coal-mining areas are the Appalachian Mountains in West Virginia, Kentucky, and parts of Ohio. Today, however, a decline in manufacturing, the closing of steel mills, and high unemployment have given the nickname "Rust Belt" to this highly industrialized region, which has seen many of its factories closed down due to lack of business. In comparison, Japanese steel production is now higher than that of the United States by about 10 percent.

Above *A print showing an early ironworks factory in New York City*

Below *A modern car-assembly line at a Chrysler plant in Detroit, Michigan*

CAR MANUFACTURING

The area around Detroit, Michigan, is the center of the automobile industry. Known as Motortown, or Motown, the industry has also given its name to the popular rhythm and blues music industry there. Henry Ford established the first assembly line plants in Detroit to manufacture his Model T, the first mass-produced, budget-priced car. Other manufacturers followed, and today there are car assembly plants all over the United States, some of which have been set up by Japanese and German car manufacturers.

26

SERVICE INDUSTRIES

Alongside the decline in heavy industry and manufacturing, the American economy has seen a tremendous increase in service industries—industries that are involved in the trade, use, and repair of goods rather than their production. Service industries include the restaurant and catering industries, hotels and tourism, retail sales, automobile repairs, TV and radio broadcasting, film production, household appliances and computer repair, insurance, banking and financial services, distribution and shipping, and training for all these industries.

The sandy shores and warm Atlantic waters have long made Miami Beach, Florida, a major tourist attraction.

New York City is the traditional home of the United States' retail clothing business, the so-called "rag trade." There, much of the nation's clothing is designed, made, and marketed to retail stores. For many years, department stores were the most important part of the American retail business, but over the last twenty years most have suffered poor sales, and many well-known stores have closed down. Much of this has been caused by the movement away from cities to enormous suburban shopping centers, where customers can do all their shopping under one roof. In addition, Cable TV offers a network of shopping channels, where people can view "info-mercials" about all types of products and services. Another home-shopping service is the catalog industry. Many retailers sell their products solely through mail-order catalogs—sending out goods to customers who have ordered and paid by mail, telephone, or fax.

Transport and Communications

Over the last fifty years, the ships and trains that were such an important part of the nation's development have declined in popularity and use, and cars have taken their place. Trains were especially important in the nineteenth century because they transported settlers to the western part of the country. Today, trains are used almost exclusively to transport freight, and the number of passengers has decreased over the last twenty years.

CARS AND THE SUPERHIGHWAY

Most Americans now drive cars. In 1993, Americans spent $93 billion on new cars. The large car-driving population is served by superhighways, which provide links from one end of the country to the other and also offer roadside services such as restaurants, gas stations, hotels, and motels. Many superhighways are maintained by money from tolls charged to drivers. The roads also provide routes for large container trucks containing freight that once went by rail.

The Golden Gate Bridge has spanned San Francisco Bay since 1937. At 4,200 feet long, it is the country's second-longest suspension bridge.

HOW AMERICANS GET TO WORK

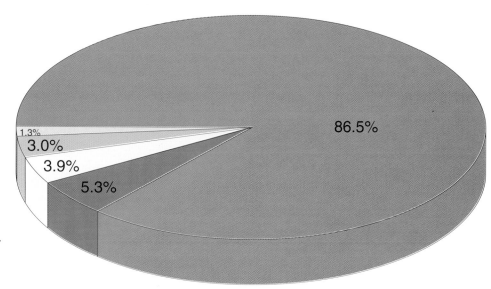

- Car, truck, or van
- Public transportation
- Walk
- Work at home
- Bicycle, motorcycle, or other means

Source: Bureau of the Census, U.S. Dept. of Commerce

86.5%

1.3%
3.0%
3.9%
5.3%

Boeing's 757 aircraft come off the production line at their factory in Washington.

AIR TRAVEL

The great distances between many cities make air travel another important method of transportation. Apart from passengers, major cargo companies carry mail and small and large packages from one part of the country to another, offering next-day delivery service.

A single company, named Boeing, based near Seattle, Washington, produces over half the planes used by airlines around the world. The first jumbo jet, the 747, was manufactured by Boeing, and since then the company has developed other generations of large planes—the 757, the 767, and, in 1995, the 777. Boeing passenger planes are popular for their safety, efficiency, and comfort. Other American companies, including McDonnell Douglas, produce the bulk of the rest of the world's airplanes and airplane parts.

29

SPACE

The United States sent some of the world's first artificial satellites into space in the late 1950s. At that time the U.S. space program was a few months behind that of the Soviet Union. Satellites have helped observers record weather and land patterns. They also provide better communication between the United States and overseas nations, and satellite dishes have brought television reception to large numbers of people in remote areas. Today, more than 6,000 U.S. satellites form a vast orbiting network in space and can pinpoint areas on the face of the globe with amazing accuracy. Infrared photography can literally see through dense cloud cover.

America's Space Program was launched in the early 1960s by President John F. Kennedy. He promised that the United States would put a man on the moon by the end of the decade. This was successful in 1969, although the Soviets

The space shuttle Discovery *soars above the clouds after its blast-off from the launch pad at Cape Canaveral, in Florida.*

had already made several important advances. In the early 1980s, the United States launched the first space shuttle. This was a craft that could be sent into space for periods of time and then returned and relaunched at a later date. The Space Program has been incredibly expensive, and many dispute its necessity. However, some of its achievements, including current astronomical observations from the Hubble Space Telescope, have proved invaluable. Also important were high-powered photographs of major planets, giving, for example, the first photographic recordings of Jupiter's moons and the surfaces of Venus and Mars.

 # Science and Technology

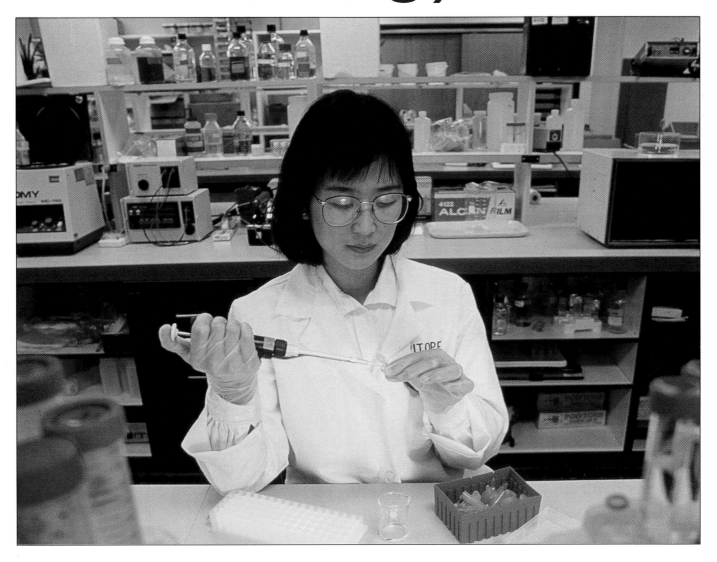

The United States is a world leader in basic research in all scientific fields, including astronomy, genetics, medicine, psychology, and engineering.

After radio, television became important to American society in the 1950s. Today, about 98 percent of American homes have one television, while 38 percent have at least two. The United States has a vast cable network system, which provides additional viewing channels and, in some areas, improved reception. About 63 percent of Americans subscribe to a cable service.

A researcher at work in a modern biochemistry laboratory

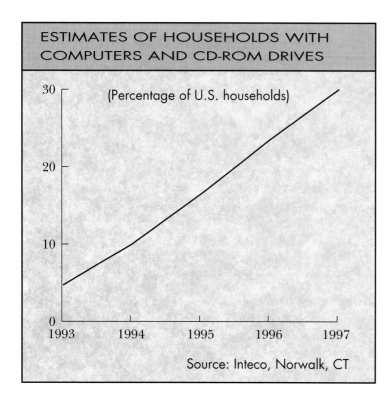

ESTIMATES OF HOUSEHOLDS WITH COMPUTERS AND CD-ROM DRIVES

(Percentage of U.S. households)

Source: Inteco, Norwalk, CT

Photography has been developed from simple home movies into sophisticated electronmicroscopy, which can electronically sense and magnify objects tens of thousands of times. Computer-imaging techniques now enhance applications in science, engineering, and medicine.

Telephones connect nearly everyone in the United States. Today's fiber-optics technology means the country can be linked to the Internet—a vast computer superhighway, which allows information to be stored and sent to computers all over the world.

A cluster of fiber-optic strands cupped in a human hand. Fiber-optic networks are the basis for modern communications systems.

"Companies like Intel [a leading manufacturer of computer chips] have done a lot of the things we all said American companies weren't doing ... investing for the long term and buckling down to really take manufacturing seriously."
—Richard K. Lester, Director of Massachusetts Institute of Technology's Industrial Performance Center

It has, however, been the computer that has revolutionized much of American society in the closing years of the twentieth century. The center of the United States computing industry is Silicon Valley, an area south of San Francisco. Headquarters for many high-tech industries and software companies are located there. The microchip, which can compress complex circuits onto one tiny computer chip, has made most of this industry possible.

The General Electric Corporation

The General Electric Corporation (GE) is one of the nation's top industrial performers and is at the forefront of technological innovation. GE was founded over 100 years ago by several pioneers of the electrical industry, including the electrical inventor and genius, Thomas A. Edison. The company grew into a multinational corporation, with thousands of manufacturing and other businesses located all over the United States and the world. Although electrical manufacturing is no longer GE's main concern, the company is one of only a handful in the world that supply power-generating equipment to electrical plants.

GE has remained successful by maintaining a tight business profile and investing in research and development. This means that there is constant pressure on employees to keep ahead of existing technology and to come up with new discoveries that are capable of changing ways of life overnight.

"Lack of computer knowledge means that companies will simply not be able to do business. To stay in business and get ahead, you have to know a lot more about computers than ever before, because they've become a key part of such things as stock control, marketing plans, sales figures and budgets, and even customer satisfaction."
—**Richard Wegener, computer expert and instructor, GE**

Life in the USA

GOVERNMENT

The United States is a democracy, with an elected president and representatives in three levels of government: Federal, State, and Local. The Federal Government's power is spread among three branches. The Executive Branch consists of the president and the cabinet; the Legislative Branch consists of elected representatives in a group called Congress; and the Judicial Branch consists of the Supreme Court. All Americans over eighteen years old may vote each year for their elected representatives at local and state level. Then, every four years, they vote for a president, who is usually a candidate from either the Republican or Democratic Party.

The Capitol Building, in Washington D.C., where Congress meets

HOW THE U.S. TAX DOLLAR IS SPENT	
Social Security	22 cents
Defense	19 cents
Welfare	14 cents
Interest on debts	14 cents
Medicare	10 cents
Health	8 cents
Veterans' benefits	3 cents
Education	3 cents
Agriculture and resources	3 cents
Other	4 cents
TOTAL	100 cents

Source: Meredith Bagby, *The First Annual Report of the United States* (HarperCollins, 1994)

WORK AND VACATION

Most adult Americans work a five-day, thirty-five to forty-hour week, from Monday to Friday. All those who work must pay a portion of their annual salary to the government. This is known as income tax. The government, in turn, uses this money to fund its work and to provide services such as education and health care for its citizens.

Most American workers get two weeks of paid vacation each year, although length of service may bring some long-term employees four weeks or more. Families tend to spend their vacations on trips away from home and often seek out attractions such as beaches along the Atlantic, Pacific, or Gulf coasts, or theme parks such as Disneyland and Epcot Center. Smaller theme and amusement parks are also big attractions.

TRAVEL

Since most Americans own cars, travel and sightseeing have become very popular pastimes. Many Americans own trailers or recreational vehicles (RVs). These "homes on wheels" allow whole families to travel in one vehicle, and they save the cost of overnight stops at hotels or motels. Popular destinations are the stunning national parks, which offer special accommodations for trailers, and the beach resorts on California's coast.

A recreational vehicle (RV) is driven through Utah's Capitol Reef National Park, one of the more than fifty national parks.

EDUCATION

Education up to high-school level is provided free by state and local governments. Elementary school, which lasts until children are eleven or twelve, is followed by junior high school for two or three years. High school begins at the age of thirteen or fourteen. This means that most children between the ages of five and eighteen years go to school for most of the year. School vacations include ten weeks in the summer and various other times during the school year. Many parents choose to send their children to private or church-run schools. Some, who dislike the lack of safety and discipline in many schools, are choosing to educate their children at home. This is becoming a popular alternative in many parts of the country, especially in rural areas of the South and Midwest.

After high school, many students choose a four-year college or university course. The cost of this education, which can be privately paid for by parents, by students with bank loans, or by scholarships, has risen astonishingly in the last thirty years. However, most states do provide cheaper

Many American schoolchildren in rural areas are transported each day by familiar yellow school buses.

alternatives in the form of state-run and supported colleges. For further education following college, such as training for professions in law and medicine, there are also some state-funded colleges, but most are private and very expensive.

There is no single official religion in the United States. Over 60 percent of Americans are Christian. These include 60 million Roman Catholics and over 100 million Protestants and other Christians. There are about 6 million Jews and about the same number of Muslims. Much smaller numbers practice Buddhism, Hinduism, and other religions.

The United States is also home to two of the fastest-growing and most influential Protestant groups—the Mormons (Church of Jesus Christ of the Latter-Day Saints) and the Christian Scientists (Church of Christ, Scientist).

The social lives of many American families still revolve around places of worship. In most areas, a number of radio and television stations broadcast continuous religious programs.

FOOD

Fast food is very popular in the United States. Drive-in restaurants have flourished as more people own cars. In addition to standard hamburgers, French fries, and soda, ethnic fast-food chains also exist selling, for example, Mexican tacos or Jewish bagels. Americans always seem to be in a hurry, and a restaurant that sells a hamburger, taco, or bagel with a cup of coffee "to go" will always remain popular.

However, in many parts of the country, traditional American foods are prepared with fresh, local ingredients. For example in Texas, beef barbecues are enormously popular; seafood is fresh and delicious near the coasts; and in New Orleans, cajun (spicy) cooking, a heritage from the original French and Creole settlers, is featured at almost every meal. American food is also influenced by both traditional British and Native American cooking, as well as Chinese, Greek, Mexican, German, French, Italian, and African-American cultures. This is reflected in the cuisine served in many restaurants.

Roast stuffed turkey and cranberry sauce are a traditional American holiday feast.

SPORTS

Americans are great sports enthusiasts, and baseball, football, and basketball are the major spectator sports. Ice hockey is also popular. Many cities sponsor professional teams for these sports, whose appearances can bring out huge numbers of fans. Spectators cheer their teams on either from the grandstands or at home in front of televisions. Golf and tennis are also popular spectator sports in the United States, especially on television.

Taking part in sports is also important to Americans, and amateur baseball teams and high-school and family football games are very popular. Physical fitness and exercise have gained popularity in recent years, with running and jogging turning many streets and sidewalks into a stream of exercisers.

A football game in a stadium in Atlanta, Georgia

HOW THE AVERAGE AMERICAN SPENDS TWENTY-FOUR HOURS	
Sleeping	455 minutes
Working	184 minutes
Watching TV and videos	154 minutes
Housework	66 minutes
Eating at home	53 minutes
Traveling to work	51 minutes
Getting dressed	49 minutes
Reading	43 minutes
Cooking	34 minutes
Child and pet care	26 minutes
Eating out	24 minutes
Hobbies	18 minutes
Shopping	16 minutes
Religious worship	15 minutes
Exercising	5 minutes
Other activities	247 minutes

Source: *New York Times*, September 6, 1995

POVERTY, EQUALITY, AND CRIME

In the past fifty years, inner cities have become pockets of poverty and crime. As they become more affluent, young professionals move out of city apartments to buy homes in the newly developed suburbs. Many workers in major cities maintain apartments in the city during the week and then retreat to second homes in the country to enjoy weekends and holidays.

Although racial segregation was lawfully banned by President Lincoln's Emancipation Proclamation of 1863, in reality segregation did not end in the South until the 1950s. Only then were black people allowed to ride in buses with white people, to sit in the same theater seats, and to enroll in what had previously been "all-white" schools and colleges. However, statistics show that the highest levels of poverty and unemployment exist among non-white citizens. Equal opportunity and positive action programs prohibit discrimination and encourage the employment of ethnic minorities. Some organizations, including the National Association for the Advancement of Colored People (NAACP), have done much to integrate housing and business. Major movements that recognize the contributions of black people to American culture (especially in music, literature, and sports) have helped raise black self-esteem. But much remains to be done to achieve racial equality.

"We committed to reform welfare because what we are doing to the poor in America is destructive and immoral."
—Newt Gingrich, Republican, Speaker of the House (of Representatives)

41

GUNS

Guns have been a part of American culture since the earliest days of settlement. Today, the National Rifle Association (NRA) has 3 million members—people who support the private possession of firearms, mainly for sport, but also for self-defense. There are an estimated 200 million firearms in the United States, and a recorded 1.2 million children under the age of eleven have access to guns at home. In addition to gun accidents, current statistics show that an American teenager commits suicide with a family-owned gun every six hours.

Crime has increased with the growth of cities, where drugs and unemployment problems are concentrated. However, the Federal Bureau of Investigation (FBI) has reported that for the three years ending in 1994, there has been a steady drop in violent crimes in cities with a population of over 1 million. In 1994 alone, the decrease was 8 percent. But these figures do not necessarily mean Americans feel comfortable about walking city streets alone at night.

"An impending wave of teen violence is facing us as the adolescent population begins to rise in America. There are 39 million children under age ten, more than we've had for decades."—James Alan Fox, Dean of Northeastern University's College of Criminal Justice, Boston

Opposite *In some states, guns are sold in stores, like this twenty-four-hour supermarket in South Carolina.*

Three Generations

Jeffrey Saunders is sixteen years old and an honors student at a high school near Saratoga Springs, New York. He has been lucky enough to travel to Europe several times with classmates. He plays in his school's

"I can hardly wait to go to college. I think I'd like to have a career in one of the professions. But I don't think I'll be a dentist."—Jeffrey Saunders, 16 years old

jazz band, studies dramatics, and, like most American teenagers, is a sports enthusiast. In the summer he plays baseball, in the winter he wrestles, and in the autumn he plays football, several knee injuries notwithstanding. Next year he'll get his driver's license.

Jeffrey's father is a 47-year-old dentist in general practice. Like more and more doctors and dentists, Bill Saunders does not have his own office, but provides his services

through a Health Maintenance Organization (HMO)—a trend of the late twentieth century. Bill wants little more than to move to Florida, where many Americans go when they retire.

Jeffrey's grandmother and Bill's mother, Pauline, is 77 years old. Jeffrey's grandfather died five years ago. Pauline lives in the family house and still enjoys getting around. She also takes pride in her three grown sons, all of whom live with their own families within an hour's drive.

Facing the Future

Like most developed countries, the United States faces many problems as it prepares for the twenty-first century. Crime, drugs, poverty, a difficult economy, concerns about the environment, and the future of healthcare are pressing issues. Pollution that begins on Los Angeles freeways and then rises to form smog over the whole Los Angeles area is a grave concern. And trees in the northern states that have died as a result of acid rain need to be replanted.

Again, like most developed countries, the United States is trying to change things for the better. However, any changes cost money, and one of the problems facing the government is the shocking size of the national debt: $5 trillion in late 1995 and still growing. Many voices that call for reducing this debt are finally being heard. They want the nation's budget to be controlled, while still allowing the country to solve its social, economic, and environmental problems.

Traffic pollutes the air above Los Angeles' constantly busy freeways.

"I'm convinced that Republicans will be in the majority for the next generation if … we don't turn our backs on the environment."—**Sherwood Boehlert, New York State Republican Congressman**

U.S. IMMIGRANTS FROM SELECTED COUNTRIES, 1993	
Total number	904,292
Mexico	125,561
Mainland China	65,578
Philippines	63,457
Vietnam	59,614
Russia	58,571

Source: Immigration and Naturalization Service, U.S. Dept. of Justice

The U.S. is home to people of many different races, who strive to live and work together as one nation.

Other countries boast of older cultures, but the United States has made newness a virtue. In just 200 years, American literature, art, fashion, and entertainment have become important in influence and stature all over the world, and American artists and performers are constantly in demand.

Every year the United States remains the destination of nearly a million immigrants from around the world. The United States is still seen as the land of opportunity in business, education, home life, and most other forms of achievement. Americans have learned to appreciate their country and are attempting to preserve and, where necessary, improve it.

"I think, with all the country's problems, this is still the land of opportunity. I think there are some serious problems, but people still want to come here. They still find the U.S. the place to pursue their dreams."
—Lia Esposito, Cuban-born immigrant and, since 1993, a naturalized U.S. citizen

Glossary

Acid rain Rain that is formed when water and chemicals mix in the air. When acid rain falls, it damages plants and soil.

Census The count of the citizens of a country to determine the country's population. A census is taken in the United States every ten years, at the beginning of each decade.

Cold War The period beginning at the end of World War II (1945), when the United States and the Soviet Union struggled for world leadership.

Colonists Settlers in a new land or country.

Contiguous Bordering another state.

Continental United States The part of the nation that is on the North American continent. It includes all the states except Hawaii and Alaska.

Democratic A type of government where the country is governed by officials elected by the citizens of that country.

Exports Products sold outside the country to bring money into the country.

Fertilizers Chemical products to improve the soil's yield.

Gross National Product (GNP) The total value of all the manufactured goods and services produced in a country, usually during a one-year period, including all the money earned from investment by foreign countries.

Health Maintenance Organization (HMO) A group that makes health services available to members at a reasonable cost.

Humid Damp and moist.

Inflation An increase in prices, wages, goods, and services.

Irrigation systems Networks of canals, waterways, or sprinkler systems for watering crops.

Pesticides Chemicals that control insect or rodent pests.

Prairies Grasslands in the Mississippi Valley of the American Midwest, with tall grasses, fertile soil, and few trees.

Recession A period of economic weakness, when a country's currency value may fall, goods may lose value, and there is a rise in unemployment.

Social Security A form of pension payment given to Americans aged over 62 years. Working Americans contribute to Social Security from their wages for this benefit, which should then be available for their retirement.

Stock Market A financial market that sells shares in the ownership of various businesses.

Strip mining A destructive, open-mining method that ravages hillsides.

Subsidies Grants given to people or private companies by a government to help a public-related enterprise.

Temperate climate A climate not subject to extreme heat or cold.

Further information

Every U.S. state has a tourist bureau, which can send you information on travel and points of interest in that state. You can find addresses and telephone numbers for these bureaus listed in any current U.S. almanac in your library.

Colonial Williamsburg, Goodwin Building, P.O. Box 1776, Williamsburg, VA 23185. Telephone: (804) 229-1000.

The Museum of American Folk Art, 2 Lincoln Square, New York, NY 10023. Telephone: (212) 977-7170.

The National Museum of the American Indian, The Alexander Hamilton U.S. Customs House, Battery Park, New York, NY 10004.

Books to read

First Person America. An eight-book series detailing the history of the United States. New York: Twenty-First Century Books.

Griffin, Jr., Robert J. *The Department of Commerce.* Know Your Government. New York: Chelsea House, 1991.

Kronenwetter, Michael. *How Democratic is the United States?* Democracy in Action. New York: Franklin Watts, 1994.

Macmillan, Bill and Fell, Gordon. *Atlas of Economic Issues.* The World Contemporary Issues. New York: Facts on File, 1992.

Scott, John Anthony. *The Facts on File History of the American People.* New York: Facts on File, 1990.

Van Zandt, Eleanor. *A History of the United States through Art.* History through Art. New York: Thomson Learning, 1996.

Videos

The Peoples of North America Video Series. A 15-tape series about the diverse ethnic groups in the United States. New York: Chelsea House.

PICTURE ACKNOWLEDGMENTS
The publishers would like to thank the following for allowing their photographs to be reproduced in this book:
James Davis Photographic 11, 13 (right), 27; Mary Evans 13 (top); Eye Ubiquitous *Cover, Title page,* 16 (top), 17, 37, 45; Hulton Deutsch 14, 15; Image Bank 6, 20 (bottom), 24, 26 (bottom), 30, 31 (top), 35, 38, 39; Impact 16 (bottom), 21, 41, 42; Carol Kane *Contents page,* 10, 12; Tony Stone Worldwide 4, 5 (top & bottom), 8, 18, 19, 20 (top), 21, 22, 23, 25, 28, 29, 31 (bottom), 32, 33, 34, 36, 40, 44; Wayland Picture Library 26 (top).

Index

Numbers in **bold** refer to photographs.

American Revolution 12–13
Asia 12
Atlantic Ocean 4, 7, 8, 21

cable communication 27, 32
Canada 4, 24
Caribbean Sea 4
cars 26, 28, 37
cities 6, 27, 41
  Boston 6, **6, 7**
  Los Angeles 5, 10, 44
  New Orleans 8
  New York City 5, 7, 27, **41**
  San Francisco 5, 34
  Washington D.C. 4, **36**
Civil War 12–13, 15
climate 5, 7, 9, 19
Cold War 16
colonies 6, 7, 12, 13, 14
computers 33, **33,** 34
cotton 8, 19
crime 41, 42, 44

desert 10
discrimination 41

Edison, Thomas A. 34
education 38–39
emancipation 41
England 13
environmental damage 25, 44
equality 41
Europe 15, 16, 24
European Union 20
exports 18

farming 18, **18, 19**
  cattle 20
  chicken 20
  citrus fruits 8, 19
  crops 8, 18, 20
  dairy 9
  logging 22, **22**
  tobacco 8
Federal Bureau of Investigation (FBI) 42
fiber-optics 33, **33**
fishing 21, **21**
Florida 4, 19, 43
forestry 22, **22**

government 36, 37
Grand Canyon 10, **11**
Gross National Product (GNP) 24
Gulf of Mexico 8, 10
guns 42, **43**

Hawaii 4, 16
Hollywood 10

immigrants 14, 15, 45
income tax 37
industry 10, 24–27
  car manufacturing 26, **26**
  coal 26
  electrical 34
  iron 26, **26**
  film 10
  paper 22
  service 27
  steel 26
Internet 33

Japan 20, 24

Kennedy, President John F. 30
Kentucky 26
Korean War 16

Lincoln, President Abraham 41

Manhattan 27
Mexico 4, 24
microchip 34, **34**
Mississippi River 5, 8, **8**

national anthem 5
national debt 44
national parks 37
Native Americans 12, 14, 19
North American Free Trade Agreement (NAFTA) 24

oil 8

Pearl Harbor 16
plantations 15, 19
pollution 44, **44**
population 4, 10, 14
poverty 41

racial segregation 41
radio 32

radio telescopes **31**
rain forest 5, 10
religion 39

satellites 30, **31**
settlement 12, 14
Silicon Valley 34
slavery 15
Soviet Union 24, 30, 31
Space Program 30, 31
sports 40, **40**
states 4, 5
  Alaska 4, 12, **21,** 22
  Arizona 10
  California 10, 19
  Maine 4
  Michigan 9, 26
  Nevada 10
  New England 6
  New Jersey 7
  New Mexico 10, **10**
  New York 22
  Ohio 26
  Pennsylvania 7
  Texas 8
  Utah 10
  West Virginia 26
  Wisconsin 9
Statue of Liberty **5**
stock exchange **24**
superhighways 28

technology 32–35
time zones 5
tourism 27

unemployment 25, 26, 42
urbanization 17

vacations 37, 38, 41
Vietnam War 16, **16**

Washington, George 13, **13**
White House **4**
work 37